# THE
# TURNING
# POINT

*Eight Encounters with
Jesus That Will
Change Your Life*

DR. ALLEN HUNT

 Dynamic Catholic

Unless otherwise noted, Scripture passages have been taken from the *Revised Standard Version, Catholic Edition*. Copyright 1946, 1952, 1971 by the Division of Christian Education of the National Council of Churches of Christ in the USA. Used by permission. All rights reserved.

Quotes are taken from the English translation of the *Catechism of the Catholic Church* for the United States of America (indicated as *CCC*), 2nd ed. Copyright 1997 by United States Catholic Conference—Libreria Editrice Vaticana.

Study Guide ISBN: 978-1-929266-62-3
Leader Guide ISBN: 978-1-929266-92-0
DVD ISBN: 978-1-929266-97-5

Design by Jessica Amsberry

Library of Congress Cataloging-in-Publication Data
Names: Hunt, Allen Rhea, 1964- author.
Title: The Turning Point : Eight Encounters with Jesus That Will Change Your Life /
Dr. Allen R. Hunt.
Description: North Palm Beach : Beacon Publishing, 2017.
Identifiers: LCCN 2017016400 | ISBN 9781929266623 (softcover)
Subjects: LCSH: Bible. John—Textbooks. | Jesus Christ—Friends and associates—Textbooks.
Classification: LCC BS2616 .H77 2017 | DDC 226.5/092—dc23
LC record available at https://lccn.loc.gov/2017016400

Dynamic Catholic® and Be Bold. Be Catholic.® and The Best Version of Yourself® are registered trademarks of The Dynamic Catholic Institute.

For more information on this title or other books and CDs available through the Dynamic Catholic Book Program, please visit www.DynamicCatholic.com.

The Dynamic Catholic Institute
5081 Olympic Blvd • Erlanger • Kentucky • 41018
Phone: 1-859-980-7900
Email: info@DynamicCatholic.com

FIRST EDITION
First printing, January 2018

Printed in the United States of America

# Table of Contents

**OUR GOAL:**
## A PERSONAL RELATIONSHIP WITH JESUS CHRIST

Man, himself created in the "image of God" [is]
called to a personal relationship with God.

*Catechism of the Catholic Church, 299*

# **ABOUT** THE AUTHOR

Dr. Allen Hunt is a nationally known Catholic communicator, Bible teacher, and bestselling author.

Allen earned a Bachelor of Business Administration from Mercer University, a Master of Divinity from Emory University, and a Doctor of Philosophy in New Testament and Ancient Christian Origins from Yale University. He has taught at Yale Divinity School, Berry College, and the Pontifical Faculty of the Immaculate Conception at the Dominican House of Studies in Washington, D.C.

On January 6, 2008, Allen entered the Catholic Church. This transition represented the culmination of a fifteen-year journey, which was encouraged by a group of Dominican sisters who began praying for Allen in 1992. Allen chronicled much of his journey in his powerful book *Confessions of a Mega-Church Pastor: How I Discovered the Hidden Treasures of the Catholic Church*, published by Beacon Publishing.

As a speaker, Allen inspires everyday Catholics to more fully recognize the genius of Catholicism, the role it's meant to play in their lives, and how to share that genius with others.

Allen's books include:

- *Everybody Needs to Forgive Somebody*
- *Nine Words: A Bible Study to Help You Become The-Best-Version-of-Yourself*
- *Life's Greatest Lesson: What I've Learned from the Happiest People I Know*
- *The 21 Undeniable Secrets of Marriage*

Allen partners with Matthew Kelly as Senior Advisor at the Dynamic Catholic Institute. The Dynamic Catholic team is dedicated to re-energizing the Catholic Church in America by developing world-class resources that inspire people to rediscover the genius of Catholicism.

Allen and his wife, Anita, live in Atlanta. For more information on Allen and his work, please visit **www.DrAllenHunt.com** and **www.DynamicCatholic.com.**

*I am honored and excited to share this time with you as together we discover the beauty of the Gospel of John. As you study and read, you will begin to see John's Gospel all around you, in everyday life.*

*Please know that I am praying for you and your journey as you seek Jesus in your study.*

*May His grace and love abound in your life.*

*Allen*

SESSION ONE:

# STUDY
# OVERVIEW

**KEY VERSE:**
But these are written that you may believe that
Jesus is the Christ, the Son of God, and that
believing you may have life in His name.
(John 20:31)

01

GOSPEL OF JOHN:
# *Introduction*

Welcome to the Gospel of John—a whole new way to encounter Jesus.

This Gospel will have some people and images that are very familiar to you. The Fourth Gospel shares many things in common with the Gospels of Matthew, Mark, and Luke. But John presents familiar people—Jesus, the disciples, Mary— and images—the cross, the empty tomb—in unique ways.

This Gospel will also introduce you to people and stories you won't meet or find anywhere else in the Bible. In John's Gospel, you will meet the woman at the well; a man named Nicodemus; the woman caught in adultery; and Lazarus, the friend Jesus raised from the dead. You'll read stories about Jesus turning water into wine at the wedding in Cana, Jesus washing the feet of His disciples, and Peter's marvelous redemption after he denies Jesus three times.

If John's Gospel is so different from the other Gospels, why was it written? To help you experience Jesus Christ. John makes that plain when he writes, "But these are written that you may believe that Jesus is the Christ, the Son of God, and that believing you may have life in His name" (John 20:31). John has met Jesus personally and wants to tell you what he has seen and witnessed firsthand.

**NOTE TO PARTICIPANTS:** *Since many participants will not receive this Study Guide until the first gathering, there is no assigned reading in preparation for this first session. The Group Leader will lay the foundation for the study and then lead the group in viewing the DVD and discussing the questions included at the end of this overview. Before preparing for session two, you will want to read this first lesson on your own in order to have a better understanding of John's Gospel.*

In other words, everything written in the Gospel of John is designed to help you get to know Jesus, the long-awaited Christ. How well do you know Jesus? Do you want to get to know Him better? Have you ever really encountered Him? Have you been waiting a long time to do so?

In this study, we will focus on eight people who encounter Jesus in John's Gospel. **Our goal, in turn, will be to personally meet Jesus Christ.** After all, Pope Francis makes that very invitation to us in his Apostolic Exhortation *The Joy of the Gospel:*

> *I invite all Christians, everywhere, at this very moment, to a renewed personal encounter with Jesus Christ, or at least an openness to letting him encounter them; I ask all of you to do this unfailingly each day.*[1]

Pope Francis reminds us that personally encountering Christ is the key to our spiritual life. That's our goal! John's Gospel introduces readers to Jesus. And it is full of people, changed by their experiences with Christ, who have a lot to teach us.

In our time together, we will study the Gospel of John by focusing on eight people (or groups of people) who meet Jesus. I pray these eight encounters help you get to know Jesus and move you to find a significant relationship with Him in your everyday life. He is our one true spiritual home.

In particular, it is important to realize that you may experience Jesus in a number of ways in this study: through your own personal preparation for each session, through the discussion time in your group, and through watching the DVD presentation in each lesson.

---

1    Pope Francis, *The Joy of the Gospel* (Erlanger, KY: The Dynamic Catholic Institute, 2014), pp. 7–8.

## GOSPEL OF JOHN:
# *Our Process*

Over these nine weeks, we will study and discuss eight personal encounters with Jesus in John's Gospel. Here is how we will prepare for each week:

## I. *Preparation for the Group Session*

Each week, you will have **two** reading assignments from the Gospel of John.

**First, you will read and study in detail one passage that shares an encounter with Jesus. Your weekly preparation for the group gathering (Sections I, II, and III) will guide you to reflect on this single passage.**

Each group session will then focus on that one passage from John's Gospel to help you dive deeper into a personal encounter with Jesus. Our goal will be to study one person's experience with Jesus in order to enrich our own relationship with Him. In preparation for the weekly group sessions, please complete the appropriate section of the Study Guide on your own.

In order to get the most out of your weekly preparation, you will find it helpful to set aside about fifteen minutes each day to work on the Study Guide. Completion of each week's full section of the Study Guide will take about ninety minutes. You will quickly discover that the more intentionally and thoroughly you prepare, the more rewarding your experience will be. God will honor your diligence and work and reveal Himself to you in new ways.

We recommend that you begin your preparation and reading time each day with prayer. Ask God to open your eyes, ears, and heart to His voice in Sacred Scripture as you read. We suggest using the Dynamic Catholic Prayer Process, which is provided for you on page 160.

**Second, you are also encouraged to read three full chapters of the Gospel of John each week in order to read through the entire Gospel (there are twenty-one chapters in total). This "Go Deeper" portion of the study (Section IV) will give you the fullest experience possible.** By reading the entire Gospel, you will get a sense of the whole picture that John is painting. Taking the time to read the entire Gospel will supplement the regular weekly preparation and group discussion times. This additional reading will be for your own personal journey and will not be discussed directly in the group session.

To guide you, in the Study Guide, each week's "Go Deeper" section will provide the three chapters to read and the simple journal question for you to reflect on: "What one thing did God say to you in this chapter?" By the end of the study, you will have gathered twenty-one touchstone reflections to refer back to from your own journey through each chapter of John's Gospel.

## II. *Group Session (approximately seventy-five minutes)*

You will need your Study Guide and Bible for each group session.

1.  **Announcements** (five minutes)

2.  **Opening Prayer** (five minutes)
    Prayer by Thomas Merton (found on the inside front cover)

3.  **Watch the DVD and use the DVD Response Sheet for notes** (twenty minutes).

4.  **Small group discussion** (twenty to thirty minutes)
    Study Guide and Readings
    Prayer and Encouragement

5.  **Closing Prayer** (five minutes)
    Prayer of a Dynamic Catholic (found on the inside back cover)

## III. *Resources*

- *The Turning Point: Eight Encounters with Jesus That Will Change Your Life*

- Bible. You can purchase The New Testament (Revised Standard Version—
  Catholic Edition) from DynamicCatholic.com.

  **NOTE:** All Scripture references in *The Turning Point* are from the Revised
  Standard Version, Catholic Edition (RSV-CE), unless otherwise noted. The
  study's author has chosen to capitalize references to the name of God in
  the translation printed in the study guide.

## GOSPEL OF JOHN:
# *Setting and Style*

The style of John's Gospel is different from the styles of the other three
Gospels (Matthew, Mark, and Luke). Often called the Fourth Gospel, the Gospel
of John is filled with symbols and interesting literary devices, including irony,
wordplay, and the contrasting themes of light and darkness, life and death.
Unlike the other Gospel writers, John portrays Jesus teaching in long sections
with symbolism, rather than in short sayings and parables. That means that the
Jesus you meet in the Gospel of John may sound a bit different than the Jesus
you meet in the other Gospels. Remember, the Gospel of John is unique, just
as your own encounter with Jesus is, or will be, unique.

As the title of the Gospel indicates, John the Apostle, the son of Zebedee,
wrote the Gospel of John. In other words, the Gospel of John is his own
first-century, eyewitness account of the life and death of Jesus.

In John 19:35, John reinforces that he is an eyewitness to these events in
the life and death of Jesus. In John chapter twenty-one, the final chapter of

John's Gospel, the work concludes with the statement that this disciple whom Jesus loved (i.e., John) "has written these things; and we know that his testimony is true" (John 21:24). It is clear that this Gospel is based on traditions and stories handed on by the disciple John and believers around him.

Interestingly, you will notice that John never uses his own name in the Gospel but instead describes himself as the "disciple whom Jesus loved," or as the "other disciple." Church tradition also tells us that after Jesus died, John lived for a long time in Ephesus and welcomed Mary, Jesus' mother, into his home.

One topic to note as you read: you will notice that John often uses the term "the Jews" to identify the opponents of Jesus. It is important to remember that the Church rejects anti-Semitism and teaches us to distinguish between the entire Jewish people and the very small subset described by John as Jesus' opponents in the Fourth Gospel.

## GOSPEL OF JOHN
# *Layout*

In general, the Gospel of John can be divided into two large sections. **The first section is composed of chapters one through twelve and is sometimes called the Book of Signs, or the Descent**, where Jesus enters the world, gathers followers, and confronts opponents. The Prologue (John 1:1–18) makes clear that Jesus will reveal God. He demonstrates in the first half of the book that He is the revealer of God. His miracles and signs accomplish that. In fact, Jesus performs seven signs in the Gospel of John that reveal His glory to human beings.

**The second section, chapters thirteen through twenty-one, is sometimes called the Book of Glory, or the Ascent.** In this portion of the Gospel, Jesus prepares His disciples in Jerusalem for His death and return to the Father. He is glorified through His crucifixion and resurrection. Chapter twenty-one (the Epilogue) closes the Gospel with Jesus' post-resurrection appearances and His words to two key disciples, one of whom is the "disciple whom Jesus loved."

Again, John's Gospel has a character of its own—the stories and Jesus' teachings are distinctly different from the other Gospels. John's Gospel does not include Jesus' famous sayings, "Turn the other cheek" and "Love your enemies," as we find in the Gospel of Matthew. Nor does it feature the memorable parables of the Good Samaritan and the Prodigal Son like the Gospel of Luke.

What we *do* find in this Gospel is a Jesus who teaches almost exclusively about Himself: who He is, why He has come, and where He is going. As a result, everyone who reads John's Gospel will directly meet Jesus in an up-close-and-personal way. He is no ordinary human religious leader; He is God made flesh. And that makes for a dynamic encounter!

**SESSION ONE:**

# INTRODUCTORY GROUP SESSION

*Video Response*

## KEY VERSE:

But these are written that you may believe that
Jesus is the Christ, the Son of God, and that
believing you may have life in His name.
(John 20:31)

**Fill in the blanks and take notes as we watch the DVD together.**

1.  John's Gospel represents a _____

    _____  _____.

    Matthew 1:1

    Mark 1:1

    Luke 1:1–4

    John 1:1–5

2.  The _____ Disciple

    At Jesus' side (John 13:23–25)

    Sharing his own encounter (John 21:24)

3.  John's Gospel has a unique purpose, setting, and style.

    John's Purpose: _____in _____

    _____

4.  In John's Gospel, Jesus teaches, "I AM."
    **NOTE:** In Exodus 3:14, God first refers to Himself as I AM, when He replies
    to Moses: "I AM WHO AM." Then He adds: "Say this to the people of Israel,
    I AM has sent me to you."

    John 6:35

    John 8:12

    John 10:7

    John 10:11

    John 11:25

    John 14:6

    John 15:1

5.  Then and Now

    We are Christians only if we encounter Christ. We can touch Christ's heart
    and feel Him touch ours. Only in this personal relationship with Christ, only
    in this encounter with the Risen One do we really become Christians.
    —Pope Benedict XVI

    As you well know it is not a matter of merely passing on a doctrine, but
    rather of a personal and profound meeting with the Savior.
    —Pope John Paul II

## JOURNAL

How do you hope meeting Jesus Christ will change your life?

**SESSION ONE:**

# INTRODUCTORY GROUP SESSION

*Beginning the Journey Together*

## GROUP SHARING

1. **Who are you?** Share your name and one thing about yourself no one else in the room knows.

2. **Why are you here?** What are your hopes for this study and the group sessions?

3. **What one area of your life do you hope is most impacted by studying the Gospel of John?**

## JOURNAL

**How is life?** Reflect on what's working and what's not working in your life.

_____

_____

_____

_____

_____

Consider your hopes, your fears, your relationships, your work, your finances, and your emotions. Write down your thoughts about how your life is working.

_____

_____

_____

_____

_____

_____

*Jesus has answers to your questions, and He offers you the best way to live. Together we will seek Him in our preparation and in these sessions. We will pray for one another and encourage each other forward. May our journeys be filled with Jesus' grace.*

## *For Next Time*

Please read and complete the Session Two Study Guide and answer
the questions.

At the next session, we will discuss the Study Guide questions and watch the
Session Two DVD.

**NOTE:** Please bring your completed Session Two Study Guide and your Bible
to the next group session.

# THE WORLD
## ENCOUNTERS
## JESUS

**KEY VERSE:**

And the Word became flesh and dwelt among us,
full of grace and truth; we have beheld His glory,
glory as of the only Son from the Father.
(John 1:14)

02

**READ:** JOHN 1–3
**FOCUS:** JOHN 1:1–18

# I. *Setting the Scene*

John has a unique way of telling the story of Jesus.

If you are a big-picture person, you will love chapter one of the Fourth Gospel. John wants to help you understand in the largest way just who Jesus is and how He came to earth. He says the Word of God will become flesh. That means Jesus will reveal God in detail. Jesus steps out of heaven and encounters the world up close and personal.

In particular, John emphasizes the divinity of Jesus far more than the other Gospel writers do. This emphasis will become clear in the first chapter. As you read, you will quickly notice that John's Gospel doesn't contain any stories about Jesus' birth—it doesn't even mention traditional Christmas images like shepherds, wise men, or the manger. Instead, John begins with the big picture. The really, really big picture. The Gospel of John begins before the beginning—before time and before creation. John starts his Gospel with the pre-existent Word of God, meaning that Jesus existed even before the creation of the world (more on that later).

**World, prepare to meet Jesus, the Revealer of God.**

*This session will feel a bit different from the others in this Study Guide. These first verses in the Gospel of John do not describe one encounter with Jesus so much as they set the stage for all the encounters to come. John himself has had a deeply personal experience with Christ, but he believes it is important to start with the biggest question of all: Who is Jesus?*

## II. This Week's Encounter—*John 1:1–18*

These verses form the Prologue to the Gospel of John.

Answer the following questions to help you reflect on what you read in John 1:1–18 of the Fourth Gospel. **TIP: Circle the questions you find the most interesting or difficult and discuss them with your group at the next session.**

1. The Gospel of John starts with "In the beginning . . ." Compare that to Genesis 1:1. Why do you think John chose to use that phrase?

2. In verses one and fourteen, John describes Jesus as the "Word." The Greek word for that is *Logos*. Here it means "God's speech," or God revealing Himself to the world in Jesus. To Greeks, *Logos* was more than just a spoken word—it was the divine reason that holds the entire universe together, giving all creation order and structure. Greeks also used this term to describe the link between our human minds and the mind of God.

What are some reasons you think John started with this "Word of God" concept rather than with the stories of the Annunciation to Mary or the birth of Jesus in Bethlehem?

3.  This is our key verse for the session:

    And the Word became flesh and dwelt among us,
    full of grace and truth; we have beheld His glory,
    glory as of the only Son from the Father.
    (John 1:14)

    Have you heard this verse before?

    This is Allen's favorite verse in the entire Bible. Why do you think he likes it so much?

Do you have a favorite Scripture verse? How did you come across it? Why is it your favorite?

4. John 1:14 helps us understand the emphasis of John's Gospel: Jesus reveals God to us because Jesus is, and always has been, God. That means He was God even before the beginning.

God became flesh. As Catholics, we call that the Incarnation (God in the flesh). The Incarnation is unique to Christianity. No other religion makes the claim that God became flesh and dwelt among us. That is a bold Christian belief.

The Gospel of John was originally written in Greek. When we look at "dwelt among us" in its original language, the phrase literally means God "pitched a tent among us," or "pitched His tabernacle among us." In Exodus 25:8–9, the tent or tabernacle represented God's presence among His people. God's glory resided in the tabernacle, much like He does today in our tabernacles for the Eucharist.

Do you believe Jesus truly is God in the flesh? How does belief in the Incarnation affect your life?

If Jesus pitched His tent next door to your house or apartment, how would you react? What would you change about yourself, your life, or your residence?

5.  The Prologue captures several big themes in the Gospel of John. Notice how John describes Jesus as light and truth. As you read John 1:1–18 in your Bible, underline "light" and "truth." These words will pop up more during your study.

6.  John 1:12 reveals that Jesus is the link between heaven and earth. "But to all who received Him, who believed in His name, He gave power to become children of God . . ."

Jesus came to us, so we could come to Him.

Look later at John 1:51 and notice how Jesus is described very much the way Jacob's ladder is portrayed in Genesis 28:12, as connecting heaven and earth: "And he dreamed that there was a ladder set up on the earth, and the top of it reached to heaven; and behold, the angels of God were ascending and descending on it!"

What do you think about this image of Jesus? Can you envision Him connecting heaven and earth as the angels of God ascend and descend on Him?

------------------------------------------------

------------------------------------------------

------------------------------------------------

------------------------------------------------

------------------------------------------------

------------------------------------------------

One saint who loved this idea of Jesus as linking heaven and earth was St. Catherine of Siena. She described Jesus as the Bridge in her famous writing *The Dialogue*. She shows how Jesus provides the bridge between death and life as He connects heaven and earth for us.

Does it help you to see Jesus as the link between you and heaven?
If yes, how so?

7. Look also at John 1:29 and 1:36. Circle the words "Lamb of God" in your
Bible. Notice how John the Baptist describes Jesus as the "Lamb of God
who takes away the sins of the world."

You probably recognize these words from the Mass. Why do you think we
say these words right before we receive Communion?

8. Read about the encounters Andrew and Philip had with Jesus in John 1:40–42 and John 1:45–46.

What do Andrew and Philip have in common?

How are they role models for us today? What do they teach us about being open to God and His plans?

# III. Just for You: Experiencing Jesus

*This section will not be discussed in the group setting. It is designed specifically to help grow your own personal relationship with Jesus.*

Imagine that Jesus moves into your neighborhood. In fact, He moves in right next door to you.

How do you feel?

Is there anything you feel you need to confess to Him? Why?

Is there anything you feel you need to change about yourself or your lifestyle, knowing that Jesus is right next door?

Now imagine that Jesus comes to visit you personally at your home. As you welcome Him at the front door, are you embarrassed, excited, proud, or scared? Do you feel any other emotions?

Do you wish you would have vacuumed or cleaned certain areas of your house?

Are there books, magazines, CDs, movies, or other forms of entertainment you want to remove from sight?

As you give Jesus a tour of your home, how do you feel when He enters your . . . kitchen? family room? bedroom?

Now imagine that Jesus accompanies you as you go about your day. How do you feel when He's with you at work or at school? At a social event or ball game?

You can stop imagining—Jesus is right here with you, every moment of every day. He has come into the world. He is God made flesh. When you see Jesus, you see God.

With this realization in mind, read your response to the previous hypothetical questions. Do you need to make some changes in your life—physically, emotionally, intellectually, spiritually?

Here is a simple way to evaluate areas of your life. In Galatians 5:22–23, St. Paul describes the following nine ways that God is active in our lives. Give yourself a score between one and ten (with ten being the highest) in each of these areas:

| | | | | | | | | | | |
|---|---|---|---|---|---|---|---|---|---|---|
| LOVE | 1 | 2 | 3 | 4 | 5 | 6 | 7 | 8 | 9 | 10 |
| JOY | 1 | 2 | 3 | 4 | 5 | 6 | 7 | 8 | 9 | 10 |
| PEACE | 1 | 2 | 3 | 4 | 5 | 6 | 7 | 8 | 9 | 10 |
| PATIENCE | 1 | 2 | 3 | 4 | 5 | 6 | 7 | 8 | 9 | 10 |
| KINDNESS | 1 | 2 | 3 | 4 | 5 | 6 | 7 | 8 | 9 | 10 |
| GENEROSITY | 1 | 2 | 3 | 4 | 5 | 6 | 7 | 8 | 9 | 10 |
| FAITHFULNESS | 1 | 2 | 3 | 4 | 5 | 6 | 7 | 8 | 9 | 10 |
| GENTLENESS | 1 | 2 | 3 | 4 | 5 | 6 | 7 | 8 | 9 | 10 |
| SELF-CONTROL | 1 | 2 | 3 | 4 | 5 | 6 | 7 | 8 | 9 | 10 |

Are you happy with your scores? Take a moment and reflect on the one area you would most like to grow forward in. You may see other areas where you would like to do a little "cleaning up" as the study progresses.

_____

_____

_____

_____

_____

_____

Silently pray and invite Jesus, the Word Made Flesh, to enter that area of your life. Ask Him to help you "clean up" that area. Each day this week, pray this same prayer.

# IV. *Go Deeper by Reading the Entire Gospel*

JOHN 1–3

This "Go Deeper" portion of the study (Section IV) is designed to give you the fullest experience possible. By reading the entire Gospel, you will get a sense of the whole picture that John is painting. Taking the time to read the entire Gospel will enrich your regular weekly preparation and group discussion times. This "Go Deeper" reading will be for your own personal journey and will not be discussed directly in the group session.

To guide you, in the Study Guide, each week's "Go Deeper" section will provide the three chapters to read and the simple journal question for you to reflect on: "What one thing did God say to you in this chapter?" By the end of the study, you will have gathered twenty-one touchstone reflections to refer back to from your own journey through each chapter of John's Gospel.

Begin with personal prayer (using the Dynamic Catholic Prayer Process found on page 160). Read John chapters one through three (the first three chapters of John's Gospel).

## JOURNAL

### Chapter One

What one thing did God say to you in this chapter?

### Chapter Two

What one thing did God say to you in this chapter?

### Chapter Three

What one thing did God say to you in this chapter?

**SESSION TWO:**
# THE WORLD
# ENCOUNTERS JESUS
*Video Response*

**Fill in the blanks and take notes as we watch the DVD together.**

1. The verse that _____ _____

   And the Word became flesh and dwelt among us,

   full of grace and truth; we have beheld His glory,

   glory as of the only Son from the Father.

   (John 1:14)

2. John's unique _____ perspective

3. When you see Jesus, you see _____

# *Journal and Notes*

## *For Next Time*

Please read and complete the Session Three Study Guide and answer the questions.

At the next session, we will discuss the Study Guide questions and watch the Session Three DVD.

**NOTE:** Please bring your completed Session Three Study Guide and your Bible to the next group session.

# THE WEDDING PARTY
## ENCOUNTERS
## JESUS

**KEY VERSE:**

This, the first of His signs, Jesus did at Cana in Galilee,
and manifested His glory; and His disciples believed in Him.
(John 2:11)

03

**READ:** JOHN 4–6
**FOCUS:** JOHN 2:1–11

# I. Setting the Scene

In chapter two of his Gospel, John tells the story of the Wedding at Cana—
Jesus' first miracle, His first "sign." Remember from our introduction that the
first half of John's Gospel is organized around seven signs Jesus performs to
reveal His glory. We'll talk in more detail about that later in this session.

As you may have guessed, no other Gospel tells this Wedding at Cana story.
Notice how Jesus attends a wedding along with His mother, Mary, and His disciples. During Jesus' time, wedding celebrations often lasted about a week, and
it was common for guests to contribute to the food and beverage selections.

When the wine runs out, Mary turns to Jesus and tells Him to do something
about it. And oh boy, does He! Jesus instructs the servants to fill six huge
twenty- to thirty-gallon jars with water. Then, He turns the water—*all* of the
water—into wine. And not just any wine, but the very best wine those wedding
guests will enjoy.

Imagine being the bride or groom at that wedding. All of your family and
friends are celebrating with you. The good times are rolling. And then, the
wine runs out. Shortage.

This first miracle story is a story of abundance. After all, as Jesus will tell us later
in John 10:10, He has come that we might "have life and have it abundantly."
The Wedding at Cana illustrates Jesus' desire and capacity to do just that:
turn our shortages into His abundance.

**Bride, groom, and wedding servers, prepare to meet Jesus, the Lord
of abundance.**

## *II. This Week's Encounter—John 2:1–11*

These verses share the story of Jesus' first miracle—turning water into wine at the wedding at Cana.

Answer the following questions to help you reflect on what you have read in John 2:1–11. **Tip: Circle the questions you find the most interesting or difficult and discuss them with your group at the next session.**

1.  John doesn't provide any details about how the bride and groom reacted "when the wine failed . . ." (John 2:3). In fact, the Gospel doesn't specifically say that the bride and groom even knew about the situation. We do know that the wedding servers discovered that the wine was gone.

    Describe how the bride and groom might have felt "when the wine failed."

    _____

    _____

    _____

    _____

    Have you ever been present for a wedding that had a huge embarrassing moment?

    _____

    _____

    _____

    _____

How do you think the wedding servers felt?

2. When the wine runs short, Mary doesn't hesitate—she immediately turns to Jesus and says, "They have no wine." Notice that Mary's first instinct was to turn to Jesus when the wine ran out.

Jesus responds, "O woman, what have you to do with me? My hour has not yet come" (John 2:4). That almost sounds disrespectful, doesn't it? But that's not the case. During Jesus' time, the term "woman" was a common and polite way to address a woman. In fact, Jesus uses it again when He speaks to Mary from the cross in John 19:26.

Here, Jesus' response really means, "Why is this wine shortage any of *our* business?"

Why do you think Jesus responded like He did?

3. We will talk more about Mary, the Mother of God, later in this study. For now, consider whether you have had a time in your life when you asked Mary to help you. Perhaps it was a time you prayed a Hail Mary.

Is it helpful for you to think about her asking Jesus to help you just like she did for the bride and groom in this story? They had a shortage, and Mary intervened and asked Jesus to help.

Is there an area of your life right now where you'd like to experience an abundance rather than a shortage? How might Mary intercede with Jesus for you?

4.  This is our key verse for the session:

    This, the first of His signs, Jesus did at Cana in Galilee,
    and manifested His glory; and His disciples believed in Him.
    (John 2:11)

    Jesus performs seven signs in the first half of the Fourth Gospel. If time
    permits, quickly read each of the additional six "sign" stories. Make note of
    what kind of shortage Jesus addresses in these six additional signs. Focus
    on how He turns shortages into abundance.

    •   John 4:46–54—Healing the official's son

    •   John 5:1–15—Healing the lame man by the pool of Bethsaida

    •   John 6:1–14—Feeding of five thousand people

    •   John 6:16–20—Walking on water
        Fear To Faith

- John 9:1–41—Healing the man born blind

  *Blindness To Vision*

- John 11:34–44—Raising Lazarus from the dead

  *Death To Life*

5. God's Glory

John 2:11 says the signs reveal Jesus' glory.

Remember from last week's session: "And the Word became flesh and dwelt among us, full of grace and truth; we have beheld His glory" (John 1:14). This means that we see the glory of God in Jesus. Jesus is God's presence among us.

When you think of God's glory, what comes to mind? How would you describe God's glory in your own words?

When you receive the Eucharist, do you ever pause and reflect that the glory of God is entering you through the Body and Blood of Jesus, the Word made flesh?

Does that make you feel differently about the sacrament of the Eucharist?

6. After this first sign, "His disciples believed in Him" (John 2:11).

Do you think it would be easier to believe in Jesus if you witnessed one or more of His signs, or miracles?

Read John 6:30; 7:31; and 12:37. Why do you think so many people struggled to believe in Jesus, even after they had seen Him?

_____

_____

_____

_____

_____

Do you remember the story of Thomas, often called Doubting Thomas? (If not, feel free to read John 20:24-29.) Thomas refused to believe that Jesus had been raised from the dead until he saw the risen Jesus for himself. Like many people, Thomas thought that seeing is believing. Can you identify with Thomas?

_____

_____

_____

_____

_____

Why do you personally believe in Jesus?

_____

_____

_____

_____

_____

Do you ever struggle with your faith in Jesus?

_____

_____

_____

_____

_____

In what area of your life do you struggle most with putting your faith in Jesus?

_____

_____

_____

_____

_____

How can the story of the wedding servers and the bride and groom help you to deepen your faith?

_____

_____

_____

_____

_____

# III. *Just for You: Experiencing Jesus*

*This section will not be discussed in the group setting. It is designed specifically to help grow your own personal relationship with Jesus.*

Think about the areas of your life: your family, relationships, work, emotional well-being, financial stability, spiritual life, and so on.

Is there a shortage in one of these areas of your life? (It might help to refer back to the spiritual self-evaluation exercise on page 28.)

Can you describe what abundance would look like in that area of your life?

Mary intervened for the bride and groom by asking Jesus to help when the wine ran out. How might Mary intervene and help you?

_____

_____

_____

_____

_____

Ask Mary to do just that—ask her to ask Jesus to help you with the shortage in one of those areas of your life; pray for His abundance. *(Suggestion: You might pray one decade of the rosary, or use the Mary prayer from Fr. Liam Lawton, found in the Additional Prayer Resources on page 162.)*

Jesus has come into the world. He is God made flesh. Incarnate. And He is right here with you.

Silently pray and invite Jesus to enter the area of your life where you are experiencing a shortage. Make that same prayer each day this week.

# *IV. Go Deeper by Reading the Entire Gospel*
JOHN 4-6

Remember: this "Go Deeper" portion of the study (Section IV) is designed to help you get the fullest experience from this study. By reading the entire Gospel, you will get a sense of the whole picture that John is painting. Taking the time to read the entire Gospel will supplement the regular weekly preparation and group discussion times. This additional reading will be for your own personal journey and will not be discussed directly in the group session. In fact, in many weeks, this additional reading will have you reading chapters of John's Gospel that do not match the session's focus passage. Remember that the goal of going deeper is to read through the whole Gospel so that you have a sense of the big picture that John is presenting.

By the end of the study, you will have gathered twenty-one touchstone reflections to refer back to from your own journey through each chapter of John's Gospel.

Begin with personal prayer (using the Dynamic Catholic Prayer Process found on page 160). Read John chapters four through six.

## JOURNAL

### Chapter Four

What one thing did God say to you in this chapter?

### Chapter Five

What one thing did God say to you in this chapter?

### Chapter Six

What one thing did God say to you in this chapter?

SESSION THREE:

# THE WEDDING PARTY
## ENCOUNTERS JESUS
*Video Response*

**Fill in the blanks and take notes as we watch the DVD together.**

1.  The Seven Signs

    Designed to reveal His glory

    Designed to convert shortages into abundances

2. The Seven Signs

    _____ into _____

    _____ into _____

    _____ into _____

    _____ into _____

    _____ into _____

    _____ into _____

    _____ into _____

## *Journal and Notes*

## *For Next Time*

Please read and complete the Session Four Study Guide and answer
the questions.

At the next session, we will discuss the Study Guide questions and watch the
Session Four DVD.

**NOTE:** Please bring your completed Session Four Study Guide and your Bible
to the next group session.

# NICODEMUS
# ENCOUNTERS
# JESUS

**KEY VERSE:**
This man came to Jesus by night and said to Him,
"Rabbi, we know that you are a teacher come from God;
for no one can do these signs that you do,
unless God is with him."
(John 3:2)

04

**READ:** JOHN 7–9
**FOCUS:** JOHN 3:1–21

## *I. Setting the Scene*

John's Gospel teems with symbols, irony, word play, and contrasting themes. Nowhere is this more evident than in the story of Nicodemus' unique encounter with Jesus (John 3:1–21).

Nicodemus was a well-educated, highly respected Pharisee. He is described as a "ruler of the Jews," meaning he was probably a member of the Sanhedrin, the Jewish high court. Even with this distinguished status, Nicodemus comes to visit Jesus "by night."

As we will see, John uses day/night and light/dark to describe more than the time of the day. Darkness represents ignorance and confusion about, or even rejection of, God's purpose in Jesus.

Nicodemus goes to see Jesus because he is seeking answers. He has seen the signs and heard the rumors about Jesus. Now he wants to discover for himself who Jesus really is. His spirit yearns to know God, even if it means he has to grow out of some old habits and into some new ones.

Jesus and Nicodemus engage in quite a conversation. During this encounter, Jesus speaks the famous words: "For God so loved the world that He gave His only Son, that whoever believes in Him should not perish but have eternal life" (John 3:16).

Most importantly, Nicodemus is changed by this conversation. We know this as we read the rest of the story in the Fourth Gospel. In the end, Nicodemus will join with Joseph of Arimathea to remove the crucified body of Jesus from the cross (John 19:39). Together they anoint and wrap the body to give Jesus a proper burial. And they are the ones who lay Jesus in the tomb.

**Nicodemus, prepare to meet Jesus, Lord of light.**

## II. *This Week's Encounter—John 3:1–21*

These verses reveal Nicodemus' encounter with Jesus.

Answer the following questions to help you reflect on what you read in John 3:1–21. **Tip: Circle the questions you find the most interesting or difficult and discuss them with your group at the next session.**

1. In John 3:2, Nicodemus "came to Jesus by night." What are some reasons Nicodemus may have visited Jesus when it was dark?

   *5-81 cat*

2. Throughout his Gospel, John uses day/night and light/dark imagery. Take a look at these verses from John and make a brief note on what John is saying in each.

   • John 1:5

   • John 3:2

- John 3:19–21


- John 8:12


- John 11:10


- John 12:36


- John 12:46


- John 13:30


- John 19:39

3.  Nicodemus wants to know more about Jesus. He has seen some of the signs and is trying to figure out the truth about who Jesus is. Jesus responds to Nicodemus in John 3:3 with the words, "Unless one is born anew, he cannot see the kingdom of God."

    The Greek word for *anew* or *again* can also be translated *above*. Since in John 3:31, Jesus is clearly speaking about coming from above, verse 3 is often translated "born from above."

    What do you think Jesus means by the statement "Unless one is born anew, he cannot see the kingdom of God"?

    _____

    _____

    _____

    _____

    _____

    _____

    **TIP: Look at John 1:12–13 and John 8:23 for additional thoughts on this idea.**

4.  In John 3:5-8, Jesus expands on the idea of "being born anew." He contrasts being "born of flesh" with "being born of water and Spirit."

    Take a quick look at these verses found later in the New Testament

    - Romans 6:4
    - 1 Corinthians 6:11
    - 1 Corinthians 12:13
    - Titus 3:5-6

    What do you think it means to be "born of water and Spirit"?

    _____

    _____

    _____

    _____

    _____

    _____

5.  You are probably familiar with the famous words of John 3:16. "For God so loved *the world* that He gave His only Son, that *whoever* believes in Him should not perish but have eternal life."

    These words reinforce what we learned about the theme of the Gospel found in John 20:31. Jesus came to give us life.

    Take a moment and substitute your name in place of "the world" in the words of this famous verse.

"For God so loved **[YOUR NAME]** that He gave His only Son, that **[YOUR NAME]** who believes in Him should not perish but have eternal life."

How does it make you feel to say these words aloud?

Does it help you experience the love God has for you? How so?

6.  Read John 3:17. Coming after John 3:16, this verse is often forgotten. Underline John 3:17 in your Bible. Circle the words "not" and "condemn." Let this remind you of God's love. He doesn't want to condemn you (or anyone in the world)—He wants to love and save all people.

    How does John 3:17 affect your understanding of John 3:16?

    _____

    _____

    _____

    _____

    _____

    _____

7.  Nicodemus shows up two more times later in the Gospel of John.

    Read John 7:45–52. What does this passage say about Nicodemus?

    _____

    _____

    _____

    _____

    _____

    _____

Read John 19:38–42. What does this passage say about Nicodemus?

_____

_____

_____

_____

_____

How do you see Nicodemus growing and changing as the Gospel story unfolds?

_____

_____

_____

_____

_____

# III. Just for You: Experiencing Jesus

*This section will not be discussed in the group setting. It is designed specifically to help grow your own personal relationship with Jesus.*

As John's Gospel unfolds, Nicodemus grows closer and closer to Jesus. First he comes at night, seeking answers to his questions. Then he defends Jesus and cautions Jesus' opponents. Finally he steps fully and publicly into the light as he and Joseph of Arimathea bury Jesus after the crucifixion. Slowly, Nicodemus moves from the "darkness" of John 3:2—"He came to Jesus by night"—into the "light" of John 19:39–42—burying Jesus after His crucifixion.

For Nicodemus, getting closer to Jesus requires courage, boldness, and even financial sacrifice. He supplies burial ointments and cloths, which were expensive at that time. Nicodemus sacrificed and risked a great deal in order to serve Jesus.

In a way, John uses Nicodemus to paint a picture of a model disciple. It takes time and effort to grow closer and closer to Jesus. It also requires the help of the Holy Spirit.

As Nicodemus encounters Jesus, he moves from resistance to inquiry to seeking to growing. He moves along the spectrum below.

**Rejection    Resistance    Inquiry    Seeking    Believing    Growing and Loving**

**DARKNESS**                                                                **LIGHT**

**Rejection:** Actively turning your back on Jesus

**Resistance:** Sensing a nudging of faith from Jesus but choosing not to act on it

**Inquiry:** Asking questions about who Jesus is and what He desires of you

**Seeking**: Taking steps to know Jesus, have your questions answered, and find ways to understand His purpose for your life

**Believing:** Knowing Jesus as Lord and beginning to explore what that means for your life

**Growing and Loving:** Placing Jesus at the center of your life, and regularly inviting His direction and help in how you invest your love, time and money. Embracing Him as your savior and the lover of your soul

Where would you place yourself on the faith spectrum?

_____

_____

_____

_____

_____

What evidence do you have that supports your current position on the faith spectrum?

Here are some ways to evaluate whether you are growing and loving:

1. Would you say you are closer to Jesus now than you were a year ago?

2. Can you see areas of spiritual fruit growing in your life?

3.  If people around you were asked about your faith, would they say there is real evidence that you have a relationship with Jesus?

What steps might you take to move further along the spectrum of loving and growing in Jesus? Could you devote ten minutes per day to have a prayerful conversation with Him? Read a little bit of the Gospels each day? Carry a crucifix in your pocket as a reminder of His presence? Perform one generous act each day as an expression of His love?

Use this space to draft a simple plan for the next week to take one specific step forward on your journey.

# *IV. Go Deeper by Reading the Entire Gospel*
JOHN 7-9

Begin with personal prayer (using the Dynamic Catholic Prayer Process found on page 160). Read John chapters seven through nine.

## JOURNAL

### Chapter Seven
What one thing did God say to you in this chapter?

### Chapter Eight
What one thing did God say to you in this chapter?

**Chapter Nine**

What one thing did God say to you in this chapter?

**SESSION FOUR:**

# NICODEMUS
# ENCOUNTERS JESUS

*Video Response*

**Fill in the blanks and take notes as we watch the DVD together.**

1.  John's _____ Gospel

2.  John 3:16-21 = The Big Picture

3.  From _____ into _____

    John 7:45-52

    John 19:38-42

4.  St. Catherine of Siena and the Bridge

## *Journal and Notes*

## *For Next Time*

Please read and complete the Session Five Study Guide and answer the questions.

At the next session, we will discuss the Study Guide questions and watch the Session Five DVD.

**NOTE:** Please bring your completed Session Five Study Guide and your Bible to the next group session.

# TWO WAYWARD WOMEN ENCOUNTER JESUS

**KEY VERSE:**
And Jesus said, "Neither do I condemn you;
go, and do not sin again."
(John 8:11)

05

**READ:** JOHN 10–12
**FOCUS:** JOHN 4:4–42 AND 8:1–11

# I. Setting the Scene

The story of Jesus inevitably arrives at the most powerful word in the English language. What is that word? *Forgiveness.*

Forgiveness was at the center of Jesus' public life and message—He forgave sinners and taught His followers the importance of forgiving one another. In the Gospel of John, we find two powerful stories about Jesus inviting two sinful women to experience a fresh start in life—to experience redemption. These two women appear *only* in this Gospel.

The Gospel of John makes plain the power of forgiveness and second chances by sharing two unlikely conversations. First, in John chapter four, Jesus encounters a Samaritan woman at the well in the town of Sychar. Then, in John chapter eight, Jesus meets the woman caught in the act of adultery, an act punishable by stoning.

We will begin in John 4:4–42. Here, Jesus' conversation with the woman at the well provides His longest single conversation with a person recorded anywhere in the New Testament. Jesus wants to give the woman at the well a gift (John 4:10). And, as we will see in our study, this woman makes for a highly unlikely candidate for such attention from Jesus.

In the same way, in John 8:11, Jesus offers the woman caught in adultery a gift: forgiveness. Even better, He offers her a new future, a fresh start.

We never learn the names of these two women. All we have is Jesus' remarkable offering of mercy and forgiveness to two women whose reputations were anything but pure. Jesus provides them both with a second chance.

These two stories also demonstrate how Jesus elevated women to a status as valued as men. He spoke to women in public. That was an unusual step: spending time with women in daylight, in public, and thereby giving them dignity like men for having been made in the same image of God.

These two stories inspire us still today. Pope Francis quite likely had these two women in mind when he wrote in *The Joy of the Gospel*, "The Eucharist . . . is not a prize for the perfect but a powerful medicine and nourishment for the weak . . . the Church is not a tollhouse; it is the house of the Father, where there is a place for everyone with all their problems."[1]

In other words, Jesus meets two women with checkered pasts. He knows all about those pasts, but He offers them each a future. And that is the story of the Gospel. Not just the Gospel of John, but the gospel of mercy and forgiveness that Jesus brings to the world. That is good news for you and me.

**Sinners, prepare to meet Jesus, the Living Water of forgiveness.**

---

1   *Pope Francis, The Joy of the Gospel (Erlanger, KY: The Dynamic Catholic Institute, 2014), p. 43.*

## II. This Week's Encounters—John 4:4–42 and 8:1–11

These passages share the stories of two wayward yet remarkable women who encounter Jesus and experience His mercy and forgiveness.

Answer the following questions to help you reflect on what you read in John 4:4–42 and John 8:1–11. **Tip: Circle the questions you find most interesting or difficult and discuss them with your group at the next session.**

1.  In John 4:4–42, Jesus talks to an unnamed Samaritan woman at a well in Sychar, a town in Samaria. This conversation is very unexpected for several reasons.

    - **She is a woman.** During Jesus' time, Jewish teachers weren't supposed to speak with women in public. But Jesus meets her in a public place in broad daylight at noon.

    - **She is a Samaritan.** Jews and Samaritans had long-standing hostility for one another. A Jewish teacher would have refused to drink from a vessel used by a Samaritan, yet Jesus treats this woman with dignity.

    - **She has a well-known, tainted past.** She was married far more than three times, which was the absolute legal limit for Jewish marriages at the time. That is probably why she was fetching water in the middle of the day when most people would have been doing other things.

    In other words, the Samaritan woman at the well is the wrong gender, wrong race, wrong religion, and in the wrong moral standing. Nevertheless, Jesus has a public conversation with her.

Describe a person today who would be equivalent in our culture's eyes to this woman. Can you envision Jesus speaking with him or her?

2.  In John 4:10, Jesus makes it clear that He wants to give the Samaritan woman a gift.

    Take a look later in the New Testament at these verses in the short letters of John which may have also been written by the same John who wrote the Fourth Gospel.

    *   1 John 4:9–10
    *   1 John 4:19

    What kind of gift do you think Jesus has in mind? What is motivating Jesus?

3. In John 4:24–26, Jesus teaches the Samaritan woman that those who worship Him "must worship in Spirit and truth." What do you think He means?

_____

_____

_____

_____

_____

_____

**Tip: The following verses might also help you interpret Jesus' words to the woman:**

- John 1:14, 17, 33
- John 3:5–8
- John 8:31–32
- John 17:17–19
- John 18:37
- John 20:22

4. In John 4:28–30, the woman leaves her water jar and runs to tell crowds of other people what she has just encountered with Jesus.

Has a highly unlikely person ever taught you about Jesus, God, or faith? Did you give attention to his or her words? Why or why not?

_____

_____

_____

_____

_____

_____

5. In John 8:1–11, Jesus meets another woman with a questionable reputation. She has been caught in adultery. What are the differences between this story and the story in John 4:4–42 about the woman at the well?

6. Read the following Old Testament verses. What is the law concerning adultery?

- Leviticus 20:10
- Deuteronomy 17:6–7
- Deuteronomy 22:22

7. This is our key verse for the lesson:

And Jesus said, "Neither do I condemn you;
go, and do not sin again."
(John 8:11)

These are life-giving, life-changing words. Jesus forgives her and offers her a future. This is what redemption looks like.

Compare this story to what St. Paul writes in 1 Thessalonians 5:23-24. How does this passage give deeper meaning to the story of the adulterous woman? What is Jesus doing?

In the same way, what do you believe God hopes and plans to do in your own life?

8. What do the powerful stories about the Samaritan woman and the adulterous woman teach us about Jesus?

# III. *Just for You: Experiencing Jesus*

*This section will not be discussed in the group setting. It is designed specifically to help grow your own personal relationship with Jesus.*

With Jesus, the past never has the last word.

Spend some time thinking about the last twenty-four hours. Reflect on the moments when you were the-best-version-of-yourself. Reflect also on the moments when you were far from being the person God desires you to be.

When you woke up yesterday, did you spend some time honoring God and listening to His voice, or were you too distracted?

_____

_____

_____

_____

_____

When you ate breakfast yesterday, did you resolve to make the day one of grace and good things?

_____

_____

_____

_____

_____

Did you experience love, joy, and peace yesterday morning when you were at home, work, or school?

_____

_____

_____

_____

_____

When you ate lunch yesterday, did you pause for a moment to reflect on the way the day was progressing? Did you look for God's presence in your life?

_____

_____

_____

_____

_____

Were you patient, kind, or generous yesterday afternoon when you were at home, work, or school?

_____

_____

_____

_____

_____

When you ate dinner last night, did you notice the hand of God working in your life through people, activities, and things?

_____

_____

_____

_____

When you were at home last night with your family or friends, did you use the time productively? Did you waste time doing things that won't help you become the-best-version-of-yourself?

_____

_____

_____

_____

When you went to bed last night, did you pause to thank God for a good day? Did you look for ways He had been at work in you and your life?

_____

_____

_____

_____

After reviewing the last twenty-four hours, do you see some times when you weren't being the person God desires you to be? Are some of these times caused by habits or patterns in your life that go back for many months or years? If so, how?

Just like Jesus gave the Samaritan woman and the adulterous woman second chances, He wants to give each of us a fresh start. Through the sacrament of Reconciliation, Jesus forgives our sins, and we can experience a new beginning.

Today is a great day to schedule your next time for confession. Find out when your parish offers this sacrament and put a reminder on your calendar.

When you go to confession, remember the Samaritan woman at the well and the adulterous woman—they came honestly before Jesus and left changed by His mercy and love. You can experience that too!

On the next page is a prayer from Father Liam Lawton that may help you prepare for confession. It can help you encounter Jesus in the same way the wayward women did in the Gospel of John.

## *Prayer of Forgiveness*

Lord, help me to be humble
For I have wandered far from
Your goodness
and lived just for myself
Give me the courage to be
self-effacing and honest

Forgive me for the times I have
imprisoned myself
In selfishness
In greed
In envy
In arrogance
In anger
In despair
In mistrust

Forgive me for falling into
Self-pity
Self-doubt
Self-destruction
Self-containment

May these times of
falling and failing
Lead me to a greater
understanding of myself
And a new appreciation of Your
infinite goodness and mercy

Unbind me
From the dark clouds that veil my
life in fear
From the allurement of empty promises
From self-satisfaction
From the paralysis of self-loathing

To be humble
Is to come close to You
Who desires nothing more only
To love us as You do

Heal the deepest places of hurt
So that nothing is hidden from You
And the gaze of Your gentle eyes

In my sorrow
May I listen to the words of those
Who seek forgiveness from me
May I accept the sincerity of their hearts
So they too will know Your healing mercy
Through my pardon

Lord, forgive my blindness
In failing to see Your abundant blessings
Given daily from Your kindness

Forgive me Lord
That I would live again.

(Fr. Liam Lawton, *The Hope Prayer*)[1]

---

1    Fr. Liam Lawton, *The Hope Prayer* (Chicago, IL: GIA Publications, 2010)

# *IV. Go Deeper by Reading the Entire Gospel*

JOHN 10–12

Begin with personal prayer (using the Dynamic Catholic Prayer Process found on page 160). Read John chapters ten through twelve.

## JOURNAL

### Chapter Ten

What one thing did God say to you in this chapter?

<br><br><br><br><br><br>

### Chapter Eleven

What one thing did God say to you in this chapter?

**Chapter Twelve**

What one thing did God say to you in this chapter?

SESSION FIVE:
# TWO WAYWARD WOMEN
## ENCOUNTER JESUS
*Video Response*

**Fill in the blanks and take notes as we watch the DVD together.**

1. The _____ _____

   _____.


2. The Most Powerful Word in the English Language = _____.


3. Wayward women = _____ like _____.

## *Journal and Notes*

## *For Next Time*

Please read and complete the Session Six Study Guide and answer the questions.

At the next session, we will discuss the Study Guide questions and watch the Session Six DVD.

**NOTE:** Please bring your completed Session Six Study Guide and your Bible to the next group session.

# HUNGRY CROWDS
## ENCOUNTER
## JESUS

**KEY VERSE:**
He who eats my flesh and drinks my blood
abides in me, and I in him.
(John 6:56)

06

**READ:** JOHN 13–15
**FOCUS:** JOHN 6:22–69

# I. Setting the Scene

For Catholics, the sixth chapter of John may well be the most meaningful chapter of the entire New Testament. This chapter, with its focus on the Bread of Life, forms the foundation for our love and devotion to the Eucharist as the centerpiece of our faith.

John chapter six begins with Jesus' performing His fourth and fifth signs, feeding five thousand people with five barley loaves and two fish (John 6:1–15) and walking on water (John 6:16–21). These miracles also occur in the other Gospels and may be quite familiar to you.

However, beginning in John 6:22, Jesus then launches into His special teaching on the Bread of Life. You will notice how most of the teaching is about who Jesus is. Jesus even uses the "I AM" sayings we have studied in session one to emphasize His divinity: "I AM the Bread of Life" (John 6:35, 48) and "I AM the living bread" (John 6:51).

The climax of the chapter, however, rests in the powerful words of John 6:51–58. We will spend most of this session focusing on these words that have inspired believers throughout the entire history of the Church, including the following:

> *St. Ignatius of Antioch, a martyr at the end of the first century:* "I want only God's bread, which is the **Flesh of Jesus Christ** . . . and for drink **I crave His Blood which is love that cannot perish.**"

> *St Jerome, fourth-century Doctor of the Church:* "It is dangerous to try to get to heaven without the **Bread of Heaven.**"

*St. Maximilian Kolbe, twentieth-century martyr at Auschwitz:* "You come to me and **unite Yourself intimately to me under the form of nourishment.** Your Blood now runs in mine, Your Soul, Incarnate God, penetrates mine, giving courage and support. What miracles! Who would have ever imagined such!"

**Hungry souls, prepare to meet Jesus, the Bread of Life.**

## II. *This Week's Encounter—John 6:22–69*

This passage, found after Jesus miraculously feeds five thousand people with five loaves and two fish and walks on the water, contains some of the most powerful and significant words of the Gospel and the Catholic faith.

Answer the following questions to help you reflect on what you read in John 6:22–69. **Tip: Circle the questions you find most interesting or difficult and discuss them with your group at the next session.**

1.  John 6:22–69 is a long passage. What three things most fascinate you or most capture your attention?

     _____

     _____

     _____

     _____

     _____

2. This passage is loaded with references to the Old Testament. Compare the following Old Testament passages with the teachings in John chapter six. What do you notice?

- Exodus 16:2–4
- Psalms 78:23–25
- Numbers 11:11–13
- 2 Kings 4:42–44

3. Jesus often appears to repeat Himself in John 6:22–69. Note briefly what He says in each of the following verses:

- John 6:35

- John 6:48

- John 6:51

- John 6:53

_____

_____

- John 6:54

_____

_____

- John 6:55

_____

_____

- John 6:56 (our key verse this week)

_____

_____

- John 6:57

_____

_____

- John 6:58

_____

_____

Why do you think Jesus emphasizes these points so much?

_____

_____

_____

_____

_____

_____

Do you see a relationship between the above verses and John 1:14?

_____

_____

_____

_____

_____

4. In John 6:11, Jesus gave thanks. In Greek, the word for "thanksgiving" is *eucharisto*, which is where we get the English word "Eucharist." When we celebrate the Eucharist, we give thanks to God.

   Compare Jesus' actions in John 6:11 to His words at the Last Supper in Luke 22:19. What do you notice?

   _____

   _____

   _____

   _____

   _____

   _____

5. In John 6:56, Jesus makes a bold promise.

   Read John 15:4-7 for an expansion of Jesus' promise. In your own words, describe the promise.

   _____

   _____

   _____

   _____

   _____

   _____

Take a look at John 14:23 and John 17:21-23. How do they further expand Jesus' promise?

_____

_____

_____

_____

_____

_____

6. Read John 6:60-66 again. Why do you think so many disciples turn away and leave Jesus at this point?

_____

_____

_____

_____

_____

Are there parts of Jesus' life and teachings that you find difficult to understand or obey?

_____

_____

_____

_____

_____

For you, what is the hardest part of being a follower of Jesus?

7.  In John 6:67, Jesus asks the Twelve, "Do you also wish to go away?" What does Peter's response mean to you?

Have you ever felt the way Peter did, as though you had no one else to go to except Jesus? If so, describe that time in your life.

# III. Just for You: Experiencing Jesus

*This section will not be discussed in the group setting. It is designed specifically to help grow your own personal relationship with Jesus.*

In John chapter six, Jesus paints a very detailed and passionate picture of the Eucharist. The Catechism calls the Eucharist the "source and summit of the Christian life" (CCC, 1324).

What do you remember about your First Communion—the first time you received the Eucharist?

Describe that day. How did you feel before, during and after Mass? Who was there? What were you wearing? Did the priest say anything to you?

In John 6:56, Jesus says, "He who eats my flesh and drinks my blood abides in me, and I in him." That is a bold promise.

With Jesus' words in mind, do one of the following things this week:

- **Attend Mass one more time than you normally do in a typical week**. For example, if you usually attend Mass only on Sunday, add one weekday Mass to your schedule this week. As you receive Communion at this additional Mass, invite Jesus to remain in you and to transform you with His divine presence in the Eucharist.

- **Spend an hour of Adoration before the Blessed Sacrament in an Adoration chapel near you.** Invite Jesus to remain in you. Ask Him to saturate every portion of your body and soul.

*The signs of bread and wine become,*
*in a way surpassing understanding,*
*the Body and Blood of Christ.*
(CCC, 1333)

## *IV. Go Deeper by Reading the Entire Gospel*
JOHN 13–15

Begin with personal prayer (using the Dynamic Catholic Prayer Process found on page 160). Read John chapters thirteen through fifteen.

### JOURNAL

**Chapter Thirteen**

What one thing did God say to you in this chapter?

**Chapter Fourteen**

What one thing did God say to you in this chapter?

**Chapter Fifteen**

What one thing did God say to you in this chapter?

**SESSION SIX:**

# HUNGRY CROWDS
# ENCOUNTER JESUS

*Video Response*

**Fill in the blanks and take notes as we watch the DVD together.**

1.  Jesus says it _____ times.

2.  We are the _____ of the _____.

## *Journal and Notes*

## *For Next Time*

Please read and complete the Session Seven Study Guide and answer the questions.

At the next session, we will discuss the Study Guide questions and watch the Session Seven DVD.

**NOTE:** Please bring your completed Session Seven Study Guide and your Bible to the next group session.

# LAZARUS, MARTHA, AND MARY ENCOUNTER JESUS

**KEY VERSE:**
When He had said this, He cried in a loud voice,
"Lazarus, come out!"
(John 11:43)

07

**READ:** JOHN 16–18
**FOCUS:** JOHN 11:1–12:11

# I. Setting the Scene

What do you think is the longest single story in the Gospel of John? It's the story shared in John 11:1–12:11.

What story could be so important? The last of Jesus' seven signs.

And what does He do in that last sign? Raises His beloved friend, Lazarus, from the dead. What a climax! Jesus doesn't do funerals. He does resurrections.

This resurrection story, and the drama surrounding it, set the stage for Jesus' own death and resurrection. Here's how the story unfolds. Lazarus dies (John 11:1–16), and Jesus shares that He is the Resurrection and the Life (John 11:17–27). Then Jesus raises Lazarus from the dead (John 11:28–44). As a result, the Jewish leaders and the Sanhedrin begin to plan to kill Jesus (John 11:45–57). Next, Mary anoints Jesus (John 12:1–8), and finally the leaders plot to kill both Jesus and Lazarus (John 12:9–11).

Jesus risks His life to give life to His friend, Lazarus, when Martha and Mary request it. As the story progresses, we see dimensions of Jesus we find nowhere else in the Gospels. We encounter a "deeply moved in spirit and troubled" Jesus in John 11:33. He even weeps (see John 11:35) outside of Lazarus's tomb.

The clear theme of this remarkable story of the seventh sign of Jesus is life. Very simply, Jesus gives life. That should not surprise us, given the fact that all things came into being through Him in the first place (John 1:3–4).

John pieces his story of Jesus together masterfully. He uses all of this drama to set up the Passion narrative. The raising of Lazarus sets the stage for Jesus' triumphal entry into Jerusalem (John 12:12–19), and then finally, in the end, for His own death and resurrection.

But with Jesus, death does not win. Jesus is life. He not only gives life, His resurrection is the main event of the Gospel and of our faith. The real lesson of life points to the theme of the entire Gospel, "that believing you may have life in His name" (John 20:31).

**Mortals, prepare to meet Jesus, the Giver of Life.**

## II. This Week's Encounter—*John 11:1–12:11*

This long passage shares Martha, Mary, and Lazarus' encounter with Jesus. It is the last of Jesus' seven signs and sets the stage for the Passion narrative.

Answer the following questions to help you digest what you read in John 11:1–12:11. **Tip: Circle the questions you find most interesting or difficult and discuss them with your group at the next session.**

1.  St. Ignatius of Loyola liked to read Scripture and meditate on it by imagining himself present in the story. Place yourself in this story, either as one of the characters or as a spectator watching the events unfold. Jesus arrives when Lazarus has already been in the tomb for four days. Describe the scene, the smells and the sounds of the village, the mourners, the cemetery, Jesus' disciples, and Mary and Martha. What are some of the emotions and feelings that those at the scene are experiencing?

    _____

    _____

    _____

    _____

    _____

    _____

2.  In this story, we encounter a Jesus who fully experiences human emotions and reactions. Read the following verses.

    *   John 11:33
    *   John 11:35
    *   John 11:38

What do these verses tell us about Jesus?

3. When Martha and Mary send word to Jesus about their ill brother, Lazarus, Jesus takes His time traveling to Bethany to see His sick friend. Jesus clearly acts on His own time.

Have you ever waited on Jesus to answer a prayer?

If so, what was that experience of waiting on Jesus like? Did it make you trust Him more or less?

4. Martha boldly responds to Jesus after He asks her, "Whoever lives and believes in me shall never die. Do you believe this?" (John 11:26).

What do you think about Martha's response to Jesus in John 11:27?

Compare her response to that of Peter in John 6:67–69.

How do you think you would have responded to Jesus' question in John 11:26? "Whoever lives and believes in me shall never die. Do you believe this?"

5. Jesus risks His own life to give life to Lazarus. Read John 3:16–17 and John 10:14–18 again. How do you see all these passages fitting together?

_____

_____

_____

_____

_____

_____

6. In the Nicene Creed, we say we "believe in the Holy Spirit, the Lord, **the Giver of Life**."

Here, in chapter eleven, **Jesus gives life** to Lazarus in our key verse:

When He had said this, He cried in a loud voice,
"Lazarus, come out!"
(John 11:43)

In John 1:2–4, all things came to be through the Word and what came to be through Him was life.

In Genesis chapters one and two (look at Genesis 1:24 and 2:7), **God the Father creates life**.

Notice how all three persons of the Trinity are involved in giving life. Father. Son. Holy Spirit. Our God is a life-giver.

What does the phrase "Giver of Life" mean to you?

List some specific ways you have experienced, are experiencing, or hope to experience God's giving life to you.

7.  In many ways, the resurrection stories of Lazarus and Jesus define the Christian faith. Someone once said, "If you don't believe in the resurrection, then you're not a believer." What do you think that statement means?

In the New Testament, we discover that Jesus appeared in His post-resurrection form twelve times in the six weeks after Easter. He appeared to the apostles several times, He also appeared to two disciples walking on the road to Emmaus. He even appeared to five hundred people at one time (see 1 Corinthians 15:6).

Do you struggle, or is it easy for you to believe in the resurrection of Jesus?

_____

_____

_____

_____

_____

The Church teaches that we will all be raised from the dead at the end of time. Paragraph 1017 of the *Catechism of the Catholic Church* reminds us: "We believe in the true resurrection of this flesh that we now possess . . . We sow a corruptible body in the tomb, but he raises up an incorruptible body, a 'spiritual body' . . ."

How does the story of Lazarus help you?

_____

_____

_____

_____

_____

Pope Francis said in a general audience address in April 2013, "It is precisely the Resurrection that offers us the greatest hope because it opens our lives and the life of the world to God's eternal future, to complete happiness, to the certainty that evil, sin, and death can be conquered. This leads us to living our everyday lives more confidently, to facing each day courageously and with commitment. Christ's Resurrection shines new light on our everyday realities. Christ's Resurrection is our strength!"

In other words, we are Easter people.

Do your beliefs in the resurrection affect the way you live your life? How so?

# III. *Just For You: Experiencing Jesus*

*This section will not be discussed in the group setting. It is designed specifically to help grow your own personal relationship with Jesus.*

As Catholics, we have an expanded view of the universe. We believe Jesus not only rose from the dead, but also raised Lazarus from the tomb. And we believe He will raise us too. That means we do not believe that our lives are defined and limited solely to this world and this lifetime. We believe in a spiritual realm that transcends this world. In fact, St. Paul says, "Our citizenship is in heaven" [Philippians 3:20 (NAB)].

One way we experience that expanded view of the universe is through our relationship with the saints. We believe that they pray for us, encourage us, and intercede with God on our behalf. We believe we are surrounded by "so great a cloud of witnesses" (Hebrews 12:1), and their prayers form a fragrance before the very throne of God (see Revelation 5:8).

Do you have a favorite saint? How did you become familiar with him or her?

------------------------------------------------

------------------------------------------------

------------------------------------------------

------------------------------------------------

------------------------------------------------

------------------------------------------------

What do you know about his or her life?

_____

_____

_____

_____

_____

_____

Do you ask your favorite saint to pray with you and for you?

_____

_____

_____

_____

_____

_____

Is there an area of your life that you would describe as dead, or needing new life from Christ? A relationship that seemingly has died? An emotional capacity that has been extinguished? An addiction that has destroyed a part of you or your life? Has greed or materialism sneaked in and robbed you of joy? Do you know your neighbors or have you shut them out? Something else?

_____

_____

_____

_____

_____

Spend five minutes each day this week in prayer for that "dead" area of your life.

Begin by reading John 10:10. Remember that Jesus desires to give you abundant life.

- Listen silently.
- Meditate on the story of Lazarus in John chapter eleven.
- Hold a crucifix in your hand and feel the contours of the body of Jesus to remind you that He gave his life in order to give you new life.
- Call that area of your life to mind.
- Then, pray aloud and ask your favorite saint to pray with you for new life and resurrection in your life.

# *IV. Go Deeper by Reading the Entire Gospel*
## JOHN 16–18

Begin with personal prayer (using the Dynamic Catholic Prayer Process found on page 160). Read John chapters sixteen through eighteen.

## JOURNAL

### Chapter Sixteen
What one thing did God say to you in this chapter?

### Chapter Seventeen
What one thing did God say to you in this chapter?

## Chapter Eighteen

What one thing did God say to you in this chapter?

_____

_____

_____

_____

_____

# LAZARUS, MARTHA, AND MARY
## ENCOUNTER JESUS

*Video Response*

**Fill in the blanks and take notes as we watch the DVD together.**

1.  We _____

    and _____

    until _____

## *Journal and Notes*

## *For Next Time*

Please read and complete the Session Eight Study Guide and answer the questions.

At the next session, we will discuss the Study Guide questions and watch the Session Eight DVD.

**NOTE:** Please bring your completed Session Eight Study Guide and your Bible to the next group session.

# PETER
## ENCOUNTERS
## JESUS

**KEY VERSE:**

He came to Simon Peter; and Peter said to Him,
"Lord, do you wash my feet?"
(John 13:6)

**08**

**READ:** JOHN 19–21
**FOCUS:** JOHN 13:1–38

# I. Setting the Scene

Remember from our Introductory Session how John's Gospel is divided into two primary sections. Chapters one through twelve make up the first section, the Book of Signs. Chapters thirteen through twenty-one comprise the second section, the Book of Glory. The Book of Signs features what Jesus did and His teaching on who He is. We now begin diving into the Book of Glory—here we will find Jesus' farewell teachings to His disciples, as well as His Passion, death, and resurrection.

From the day Jesus calls Peter (John 1:40–42) to the night Peter denies Jesus three times (John 18:15–18, 25–27), Peter plays a major role in the Gospel. And Peter's encounters with Jesus teach us a lot about our Lord and ourselves.

John chapter thirteen begins with the Last Supper. But notice how John 13:1–20 centers on Jesus' washing the disciples' feet instead of focusing on Jesus' words and the breaking of the bread like the other Gospels do. Peter simply cannot believe that this foot-washing is happening. So he resists Jesus' humble act of service and receives a powerful lesson in leadership.

During Jesus' time, it was customary for a host to offer water for traveling guests to wash their own dry, dirty, cracked feet. Occasionally, the host would provide a slave to wash the weary guests' feet. But the host would never do the actual foot-washing himself. To Peter's bewilderment, Jesus flips that model on its head.

This foot-washing encounter lays the foundation for Peter's future as a leader—the Rock—in the birth of the Church.

**Believers, prepare to meet Jesus, the donkey-riding, foot-washing Lord.**

## II. *This week's Encounter—John 13:1–38*

This passage shares Peter's encounter with Jesus and is full of failure, disappointment, redemption, and leadership.

Answer the following questions to help you digest what you read in John 13:1–38. **Tip: Circle the questions you find most interesting or difficult and discuss them with your group at the next session.**

1.  Chapter thirteen begins the Book of Glory, the second half of John which describes Jesus' farewell teachings to the disciples and the story of His Passion, death and resurrection. Read the following verses. Write down what you see as the key theme and purpose for each farewell teaching.

    •   John 13:1, 34; 15:12–13

    _____

    •   John 14:1–6

    _____

    _____

    •   John 14:15–17

    _____

    _____

    •   John 17:20–24

    _____

    _____

2. John 13:1–20 is John's description of the Last Supper. How is this version different from the Last Supper story in the other Gospels? It may be helpful to read Matthew 26:17–24 or Luke 22:7–23 for a comparison.

3. Unlike Matthew's, Mark's, and Luke's accounts, John's Last Supper story emphasizes how Jesus washes His disciples' feet.

   Considering how unusual and shocking this would have been during Jesus' time, why do you think Jesus chose to do that humiliating act?

   Can you think of any examples of modern leaders performing a comparable act or leading with a "servant" attitude?

Describe the best example of servant leadership you have personally witnessed in the past week.

4. This is our key verse for the week:

He came to Simon Peter; and Peter said to Him,
"Lord, do you wash my feet?"
(John 13:6)

Why do you think Peter resists and feels uncomfortable with Jesus washing His disciples' feet (John 13:6–10)?

Have you ever been served by someone and felt humbled by it? If so, how did you respond?

5. Not long after the Last Supper and foot-washing, Peter denies Jesus three times.

Read John 13:36–38; John 18:15–18; and John 18:25–27.

Have you ever had an embarrassing failure? Did other people know about it? Describe what that felt like. How did you try to overcome that failure and move forward?

6. Now read John 20:1–10. What do you notice about Peter as he goes to the empty tomb?

7. After Peter goes to the empty tomb, he only appears one more time in John's Gospel. Read John 21:1–19 and describe Peter's role in Jesus' resurrection appearance to His disciples.

What does Jesus say to Peter? Why do you think Jesus says these things to Peter?

How do you think Peter feels as Jesus speaks to him?

_____

_____

_____

_____

_____

# III. Just for You: Experiencing Jesus

*This section will not be discussed in the group setting. It is designed specifically to help grow your own personal relationship with Jesus.*

Peter goes through a host of emotions and experiences in all the Gospels. He is heroic; he is childish. He bravely leads; he stumbles in humiliation. Jesus praises Peter; Jesus rebukes Peter.

Peter was not perfect. At times he lived up to Jesus' hopes and dreams for his life. At other times, he was far from fulfilling his potential as a person and as a leader. Peter resembles us on our own faith journeys, doesn't he?

List some times in your faith journey when you really felt you were living the way Jesus called you to live—times when you experienced the fullness of your potential as a person and as a believer.

List some times in your faith journey when you stumbled or made mistakes—times when you were embarrassed by your words, actions, or treatment of others.

Read aloud Jesus' words to Peter in John 21:15–17. Listen to Jesus' words of redemption and restoration. Even after Peter denies knowing Him, Jesus restores Peter and endorses him for a new future of leadership.

Meditate on these words of redemption.

Listen for God's own blessing in your life.

Allow the Holy Spirit to enter your soul and breathe into it the healing words of Jesus. He has a plan and a purpose in mind for you.

Embrace your destiny.

**Resolve to perform an act of servant leadership at least one time this week.** Selflessly serve those around you, especially someone who is hurting or in need. As you serve, call to mind the model of the donkey-riding, foot-washing Lord. Invite Him to draw near to you as you serve in His name.

It may prove helpful for you to journal about this experience. The simple Jesus prayer by Fr. Liam Lawton can be useful as well and is provided in the Additional Prayer Resources section on page 164.

# IV. Go Deeper by Reading the Entire Gospel
## JOHN 19–21

Begin with personal prayer (using the Dynamic Catholic Prayer Process found on page 160). Read John chapters nineteen through twenty-one (the Gospel of John's version of the Passion Narrative of Jesus).

## JOURNAL

### Chapter Nineteen
What one thing did God say to you in this chapter?

### Chapter Twenty
What one thing did God say to you in this chapter?

**Chapter Twenty-One**

What one thing did God say to you in this chapter?

**SESSION EIGHT:**

# PETER ENCOUNTERS JESUS

*Video Response*

**Fill in the blanks and take notes as we watch the DVD together.**

1. What's your _____ ?


2. We follow a _____, _____ Lord.


3. Peter = The most successful _____ of all time.

# *Journal and Notes*

## *For Next Time*

Please read and complete the Session Nine Study Guide and answer the questions.

At the next session, we will discuss the Study Guide questions and watch the Session Nine DVD.

**NOTE:** Please bring your completed Session Nine Study Guide and your Bible to the next group session.

# MARY
# ENCOUNTERS
# JESUS

**KEY VERSE:**

Then He said to the disciple, "Behold, your mother!"
And from that hour the disciple took her to his own home.
(John 19:27)

09

**FOCUS:** JOHN 19:25-30

# *I. Setting the Scene*

As we've learned from the previous sessions, John's Gospel is very different from the other Gospels. And the Gospel of John's unique point of view is most obvious in two important (and exclusive) stories about Mary's encounter with Jesus and her role in the Church.

In an earlier session, we studied the Wedding at Cana (John 2:1-12)—the first time we see Mary's encounter with Jesus in this Gospel. Remember how Mary interceded for the bride and groom and asked Jesus to do something about the shortage of wine at the wedding feast.

In John 19:25-27, we read about Mary's second encounter with Jesus as she stands at the foot of Jesus' cross. In His final moments, Jesus entrusts His mother to John, His beloved disciple. In this story, John represents all of Jesus' followers. He represents you and me. When Jesus says to Mary, "Woman, behold your son!" (John 19:26), and to His beloved disciple, "Behold your mother!" (John 19:27), Mary becomes the mother of the Church and the mother of us all. She continues to ask Jesus to help us in our times of need.

As you have read John's Gospel, did you notice that the Fourth Gospel never mentions Mary by name? She is simply referred to as "woman" and "His mother." Since the Gospel of John emphasizes that Jesus is God, the name "His mother" makes it very clear that Mary is the Mother of God. What a powerful encounter—we have saved the best for last!

**Mary, prepare to meet Jesus, the Word made Flesh through your womb.**

## *II. This Week's Encounter—John 19:25–30*

These verses record Jesus' last words to His mother, His last breath, and His death on the cross.

Answer the following questions to help you digest what you read in John 19:25–30. **Tip: Circle the questions that are most interesting or difficult for you so that you can explore these more when your group discussion occurs at the next session.**

1. All of chapter nineteen focuses on the crucifixion of Jesus. It will be helpful to read the whole chapter and notice the details John provides as he shares this painful story.

   John 19:17—Jesus carries the cross Himself. He is alone.

   John 19:19–20—Pilate places an inscription on the cross, written in three languages: Greek (the dominant language of the day, particularly used in commerce), Hebrew (the language of the Jews, particularly used in religious matters), and Latin (the language of the Roman Empire and the language of legal affairs). It is from this inscription that we get "INRI," usually inscribed on crucifixes in Catholic parishes. These four letters represent the first letter of each Latin word in "Jesus of Nazareth, the King of the Jews."

   John 19:24—John's Gospel refers to Psalms 22:19 to explain why the soldiers cast lots for Jesus' seamless tunic.

   John 19:30—Jesus bows His head and "gave up His spirit." This can be understood in two ways. First, Jesus gives up the spirit of His earthly existence. In other words, He dies with that last breath. Second, Jesus hands over the Holy Spirit to His believers. Take a look at John 7:39; 14:15–20; 14:25–29; and 20:21–23.

John 19:30—In Greek, Jesus' last word is tetelestai, which is translated, "It is finished." This single Greek word can also be translated, "It is complete," or, "It is perfected." For more depth, look at the use of the same word in John 4:34; 5:36; and 17:4.

Now that you have read the entire Gospel of John, what do you think Jesus means by this final word?

---------------------------------------------------------------

---------------------------------------------------------------

---------------------------------------------------------------

---------------------------------------------------------------

---------------------------------------------------------------

---------------------------------------------------------------

2. Imagine you are Mary, the Mother of Jesus. Place yourself in this story— you are standing at the foot of the cross and witnessing the death of your only son. You are faithful all the way to the end. Describe the scene Mary witnesses. Try to imagine the memories she is recalling. Consider how Mary feels and the emotions that come to the surface.

---------------------------------------------------------------

---------------------------------------------------------------

---------------------------------------------------------------

---------------------------------------------------------------

---------------------------------------------------------------

---------------------------------------------------------------

3. This is our key verse for the week:

Then He said to the disciple, 'Behold, your mother!'
And from that hour the disciple took her to his own home.
(John 19:27)

In John 19:25–27, in His last moments, Jesus entrusts Mary, His mother, to His beloved disciple. Although John's Gospel never explicitly names the beloved disciple, it is believed that he is likely John the Apostle, the author of the Fourth Gospel. But his identity is not as important as the act itself. Jesus hands His own mother, Mary, over to the disciple and to the Church. Tradition says that Mary went to live with John, and stayed with him during the time he oversaw the churches in Asia from his home near Ephesus. Pilgrims still visit that home site each year, especially since Mary may have spent her final days on earth there.

What does this action of Jesus mean to you?

_____

_____

_____

_____

_____

_____

Do you consider Mary to be your Mother as a believer?

_____

_____

_____

_____

_____

4.  Mary is the mother of the Church and the mother of us all.

    Return now to the first time we meet Mary in the Fourth Gospel. Review the story of the wedding in Cana of Galilee (John 2:1-11). Notice how Jesus addresses Mary in the same way (as "woman") in both stories (see John 2:4 and 19:26). This term is a normal, respectful way of addressing a woman at that time.

    Notice also that at Cana (John 2:4) Jesus says His hour has not yet come. In John chapter nineteen, His hour has clearly arrived. In fact, it began in John 13:1. The hour of Jesus' glorification has arrived. That's because it is in the cross, not in any sign or miracle, that we encounter Jesus most deeply. At the cross, His sacrifice is made complete.

    As you read John chapter two again, notice how Mary intercedes when the wedding party runs out of wine. She knows that Jesus can do something about that shortage. Jesus' mother knows what Jesus can do, and she can encourage Him to do that. She is the Mother of God.

Do you see Mary as your intercessor? As your advocate? As someone who will encourage Jesus to help you and love you? Why or why not?

---
---
---
---
---

Have there been moments in your life when you have felt or seen Mary's presence or help? If so, describe one of those moments.

---
---
---
---
---

5. Mary has many names and titles. Here are just a few of the ways we address her.

- Mother of Christ
- Mother of divine grace
- Mother most pure
- Mother undefiled
- Mother most amiable
- Mother most admirable
- Mother of good counsel
- Mother of our Creator
- Mother of our Savior
- Ark of the covenant
- Gate of heaven

Do you have a name or title for Mary that is especially meaningful to you? If so, why is that name special?

_____

_____

_____

_____

_____

_____

6. Often, our relationships with our own family, particularly with our mother and father, shape our relationship with God. Reflect on how this may or may not be true in your own relationships with your parents and with God. Do you see any connections between how you related to your mother or father with how you relate to God or to Mary?

7. In this story, we also encounter "the other disciple," or the "beloved disciple." It seems most likely that he is the apostle John, the author of this Fourth Gospel. Take a look at the passages listed below and think about this fascinating character in the Gospel. He had his own very powerful experiences with Jesus, and those experiences form the foundation of his writing.

- John 13:23–25
- John 18:15–16
- John 19:26–27
- John 20:1–10
- John 21:7, 20–24

**NOTE:** If you would like to further explore the Gospel of John and its history—author, setting, dates, and other details—please visit **dynamiccatholic.com/ExploreJohn** to receive a short list of helpful scholarly resources.

# III. Just for You: Experiencing Jesus

*This section will not be discussed in the group setting. It is designed specifically to help grow your own personal relationship with Jesus.*

Mary's encounter with Jesus is obviously one of a kind. She alone is His mother. Yet, as Catholics, we believe Mary loves us and knows us and continues to do so from her place in heaven. We believe she desires to help us in our faith and our lives. We believe she intercedes for us—she encourages Jesus to help us. And, as she said to the wedding servants at Cana, she tells us to "Do whatever He tells you" (John 2:5).

How might you grow forward one step in your relationship with, and devotion to, Mary, Mother of God?

_____

_____

_____

_____

_____

Here are some ideas to get you started:

**Place a statue or picture of Mary somewhere in your home** or office as a visual reminder of her desire to serve as your spiritual Mother.

**Pray part (or all) of the rosary one day this week.** Focus on Mary and her role in Jesus' life, the Church, and your faith.

**Use the Mary prayer by Fr. Liam Lawton one time this week.** This prayer is provided in the Additional Prayer Resources on page 162.

## *IV. Go Deeper by Reading the Entire Gospel*

Congratulations! You have completed your reading of the entire Gospel of John. Look back through your notes on how God has spoken to you through each chapter.

### JOURNAL

What one thing most stands out about how God has been prompting you through this entire reading of John's Gospel?

## *V. Moving Forward*

Congratulations! You've read the entire Gospel of John, studied it, and discovered a wide variety of people who met Jesus.

1.  How has this experience shaped your own journey and experience of Jesus?

2.  What is one excellent next step you can take to deepen your faith and love for Jesus? What's the next right thing to do? How can you make this next step a reality?

3. This nine-week journey has helped you experience Jesus. Early in our study, we discovered how Philip and Andrew helped lead other people to Jesus (John 1:40-46). What is one thing you can do to help another person encounter Jesus?

Here are some ideas to get you started:

- Pray specifically each day for one person you know who would benefit from an encounter with Jesus.

- Share a copy of your favorite faith-centered book with another person. Free and low-cost resources for this can be found at **dynamiccatholic.com/MyTurningPoint**.

- Form a new small group and lead the participants through this Gospel of John study, *The Turning Point*.

**SESSION NINE:**

# **MARY** ENCOUNTERS JESUS

*Video Response*

**Fill in the blanks and take notes as we watch the DVD together.**

1.  Mary, our _____


2.  Mary, our _____


Here are some ideas to get you started:

*   Pray specifically each day for one person you know who would benefit from an encounter with Jesus.

*   Share a copy of your favorite faith-centered book with another person. Free and low-cost resources for this can be found at **dynamiccatholic.com/MyTurningPoint**.

*   Form a new small group and lead the participants through this Gospel of John study, *The Turning Point*.

## *Journal and Notes*

## Next Steps

I pray that reading John's Gospel and sharing in this study have helped you deepen your faith. Even more, in the spirit of Pope Francis, I pray that you have encountered Jesus in a fresh, life-giving way.

As you move forward in your faith journey, continue to use the prayers provided in this Study Guide. In particular, I invite you to make the Dynamic Catholic Prayer Process a part of your daily life.

Remember what Philip and Andrew did in John chapter one. Remember what the Samaritan woman did in John chapter four. And remember why John wrote this Gospel. They all desired to share with other people the incredible things Jesus did in their lives.

Pope Francis has invited us all to be missionary disciples. And that is what missionary disciples do: share what Jesus has done in their lives.

May Christ Jesus fill your life with abundance, both now and forever. And may you share that good news with the people you know, meet, and love.

Grace and Peace,
Allen

"Great is the mystery of the faith!" The Church professes this mystery in the Apostles' Creed . . . This mystery, then, requires that the faithful believe in it, that they celebrate it, and that they live from it in a vital and personal relationship with the living and true God.
(CCC, 2558)

# ADDITIONAL
## RESOURCES
**for your PRAYER LIFE**
**as you JOURNEY through**
**the GOSPEL of JOHN**

# *The Dynamic Catholic Prayer Process*

Here is the basic Prayer Process that our team at Dynamic Catholic uses and suggests as a starting point for building your own prayer relationship with God. Matthew Kelly developed this simple process after studying hundreds of prayer styles and disciplines from many Catholic spiritualities. Again, the point is forming a simple, regular habit, five to ten minutes a day. Daily prayer IS your relationship with God.

**1. Gratitude** – Begin by thanking God in a personal dialogue for whatever you are most grateful for today.

**2. Awareness** – Revisit the times in the past twenty-four hours when you were and were not the-best-version-of-yourself. Talk to God about these situations and ask Him to give you the gift of greater awareness when similar situations arise in the future.

**3. Significant Moments** – Identify something you experienced today and explore what God might be trying to say to you through that event.

**4. Peace** – Ask God to forgive you for any wrong you have committed (against yourself, another person, or Him) and fill you with a deep and abiding peace.

**5. Freedom** – Talk to God about how He is inviting you to change your life so you can experience the freedom that comes from knowing that who you are, where you are, and what you are doing makes sense. Is He inviting you to rethink the way you do things? Is God asking you to let go of something or someone? Is He asking you to hold on to something or someone?

**6. Pray for Others** – Pray for those you feel called to pray for today, and those who have asked you to pray for them recently. Take a moment and pray for these people by name, asking God to bless and guide them.

**Finish by praying the Our Father.**

## *Mary*

I have always imagined you to be young
With serene beauty
Sun-kissed face that searched the heavens
With questions only deep
Within your heart
With great love you carried your child
Watching Him grow beneath the
moon of Israel
And under Egypt's stars

You took the splinters from His
dusty hands
Turning wood on Joseph's bench
And held Him close when he spoke
of things
You could only carry in your heart

Did you know what lay ahead?
How He would heal the sick
Raise the dead
Find the lost and
See the hungry fed?
Little children would be well again
The blind would see
Lazarus would rise
And the lame run free

Did you know that your heart
would break?
When He was bound and beaten
Hung upon a tree
For all the world to see
The sin of humanity
Did your heart almost burst
When you heard the tomb was empty?
Did you run to see
And cry again so many tears of joy?

In Heaven you do not age
And you are forever young
You are beautiful
Because you love
May we know that love
In protection
In affection
In direction
Just as you watched over your own Son
Watch over us

Help us to find
That pure place in our heart
Beyond cynicism
Beyond hate
Beyond fear

Turn your gentle face towards us
That we might listen to your
Cana words
'Do as He tells you'

May we walk one day
When life is done
Through the fields of paradise
Forever young
Enfolded in your mystery
O woman clothed in the sun.

(Fr. Liam Lawton, *The Hope Prayer*)

1    Fr. Liam Lawton, *The Hope Prayer* (Chicago, IL: GIA Publications, 2010)

# *Jesus*

I come before you
In these sacred moments
Opening the shutters of my heart
That You would call the light into
the dark
The secret cavern of my soul

If I tell You who I am
Will you shelter me
Beneath the firm arms of your
compassion
And gaze tenderly
Beyond the limits of my silence?

Who am I?

I am the son, the prodigal one
Returning from my journey
Of untold wrong
Where love was scarce
And temptation strong
Can You embrace me yet again?
I am the woman at the well
Tired and weary
Longing to quench my thirst
Drawing deep to find
Your truth as well

I am the blind one
By the pool of Siloam
Can You stir the waters so I will see
Your gentle eyes
That find the light in me?

I am the weak one
Waiting for years
But I knew You would come
So I might touch the hem of Your garment
And live again

I am the curious one
Gathering to listen with the crowd
Bringing bread and fish
That You break and bless
And all become Your guests

I am the sinner
They all know my sins
I see the stones
My accusers bring
What words You write in sand
One by one I see them stand
And walk away
From what is written on each heart

I am Lazarus, friend
Wrapped in the cloths of death
When You saw me
You wept
You have called me from my tomb
And I will live again

I am Nicodemus of the night
Preferring dark to light
You have sought me out
I long for life

I am the little child
Who lies in fever's sleep
I hear You call beyond death's reach
'Talitha Koum'
Little one – come forth

Your voice is more beautiful than the
Sweetest music
It resonates forever in my heart
I am all and I am more
I hear You knocking
On my door
Your lantern burning bright
Casting shadows where my life
Still seeks Your healing touch

Jesus
The beginning and the end
Jesus
I long to call you friend

(Fr. Liam Lawton, *The Hope Prayer*)[1]

1    Fr. Liam Lawton, *The Hope Prayer* (Chicago, IL: GIA Publications, 2010)

Additional Resources

# Notes

# Notes